OUTRAGEOUS JAPANESE

SLANG, CURSES & EPITHETS

by Jack Seward

TUTTLE PUBLISHING
Boston • Rutland, Vermont • Tokyo

Published by Tuttle Publishing
an imprint of Periplus Editions (HK) Ltd..
with editiorial offices at 153 Milk Street, Boston, MA 02109

© 1991 by Charles E. Tuttle Publishing Co., Inc.

LCC Card No. 91-65059
ISBN 0-8048-1694-8

Distributed by:

Japan
Tuttle Publishing
Yaekari Building, 3rd Floor
5-4-12 Osaki, Shinagawa-ku, Tokyo 141-0032
Tel: (03) 5437 0171; Fax: (03) 5437 0755
Email: tuttle-sales@gol.com

North America, Latin America & Europe
Tuttle Publishing, 364 Innovation Drive
North Clarendon, VT 05759-9436
Tel: (802) 773 8930; Fax: (802) 773 6993
Email: info@tuttlepublishing.com
www.tuttlepublishing.com

Asia-Pacific
Berkeley Books Pte. Ltd.
130 Joo Seng Road, #06-01/03, Singapore 368357
Tel: (65) 6280 1330; Fax: (65) 6280 6290
Email: inquiries@periplus.com.sg
www.periplus.com

04 06 08 09 07 05
8 10 12 13 11 9

Printed in Singapore

✳ Contents

7

❋ Introduction

It is often taken as an article of faith that the amiable, soft-spoken Japanese seldom resort to verbal abuse or defamation in their dealings with others. All the same, while I was attending Japanese language school, our top-priority mission was acquiring the vocabulary needed to (a) roundly malign others, and (b) become cozy with Oriental maidens when we at last reached the distant, misty shores of Japan. The harvest of the second task was indeed much more bountiful than the first.

But I persevered and at length came to understand that the Japanese language—if not a cornucopia of curses and censure—is at least rich enough to reasonably satisfy occasional compulsions to condemn and recriminate.

Granted, the Japanese strive for surface harmony and try to avoid antagonistic confrontations when possible. As a result, quantitatively speaking, they do not generate verbal vitriol in the quantity or variety that can be attributed to some other nationalities. But this is not to suggest that they

9

are without their resources. As you will see herein, they can be inventive users of invective that is both vivid and injurious.

Before you begin this adventure in aspersion, let me refresh your memory about what really effective malediction sounds like in English.

The *Harper's Weekly* once reviled president Abraham Lincoln in these words:

> "Filthy storyteller, despot, liar, thief, braggart, buffoon, usurper, monster, Ignoramus Abe, Old Scoundrel, perjurer, robber, swindler, tyrant, field-butcher, land-pirate."

Reading such a diatribe, the reader might be tempted to feel sorry for poor old Abe, saddled as he was with Marfan's syndrome and a vicious harpy of a wife. Surely there are politicians teeming underfoot today who are more richly deserving of such disparagement than Lincoln was.

Or consider what Martin Luther wrote about Henry VIII of England:

> ". . . a pig, an ass, a dunghill, the spawn of an adder, a basilisk, a lying buffoon, a mad fool with a frothy mouth, a lubberly ass . . . a frantic madman."

In more recent times (1953), East German Communists serving as spokesmen of their government aspersed Englishmen in general in these pejorative terms:

> "Paralytic sycophants, effete betrayers of humanity,

carrion-eating servile imitators, arch-cowards, and collaborators, gang of women murderers, degenerate rabble, parasitic traditionalists, playboy soldiers, conceited dandies."

Although not really in the same class, the Japanese have been known to besmirch others with broadsides that should at least get the attention of the party denigrated. Author Yukio Mishima once anathematized Japanese intellectuals with this bit of vituperation:

". . . their cowardice, sneering 'objectivity,' rootlessness, dishonesty, flunkeyism, mock gestures of resistance, self-importance, inactivity, talkativeness, and readiness to eat their own words."
(Quoted in *The Life and Death of Yukio Mishima,* by Henry Scott Stokes)

However they stack up against their foreign competitors, the Japanese certainly have sufficient weapons in their armory to offend and discredit those they feel need lambasting.

✳ Guide to Pronunciation

Japanese vowels are always pronounced the same:

a	like the *a* in father
e	like the *e* in egg
i	like the *e* in me
o	like the *o* in oh
u	like the first *u* in Zulu

You will find macrons (lines) over some vowels. Differentiating between "long" and "short" vowels is important. Saying *kuso* instead of *kusō* or *komon* instead of *kōmon* will evince laughter, incomprehension, or embarrassment.

There are only two other sounds that may require some effort to master:

tsu   Place the tip of your tongue behind your

13

upper front teeth and say the girl's name "Sue."

r   This is a lightly tapped *r* which lies between the English *r* and *d*.

Although there is a slight pitch in Japanese, you should utter all your Japanese words and sentences in an even tone like the tick-tock-tick-tock of a metronome. The final *u* in the *-masu* form of verbs and *desu* is usually silent.

For a more detailed discussion of pronunciation, see *Japanese in Action* and *Learning Basic Japanese* by the same author.

OUTRAGEOUS JAPANESE

ONE

Ridiculing Physical Appearance

Fat or Skinny

The Japanese language is rich in words to hurt others through disparaging comments about weight, shape, age, attire, odor, and hairiness. Let's look first at several choice words of abuse that can be directed at those who are, bluntly speaking, *futotte iru* (fat). There is a very good (and obvious) reason that I know a god's plenty of such colorful epithets, enough of them having been directed at my person.

I must note, however, that the Japanese may not all agree that such words are belittling. Although the younger generation wants to be "smart" (meaning fashionably slender, not intelligent), the older ones tend to regard obesity as obvious proof of success and wealth. Else, how could you afford to eat enough to put on that extra weight? Indeed, the word for paunch is *jūyaku-bara,* or "a company director's stomach."

I shudder to recall how often a Japanese acquaintance (I disdain to use the word friend) has launched at me a brutal barb like:

Mā, Suwādo-san wa hontō ni futotte iru, ne. — You really are fat, aren't you, Mr. Seward.

I try to keep in mind that my acquaintance may have meant his comment as a compliment of sorts but it has taken me a long time to accustom myself to such frank evaluation, a very long time indeed.

Other words which can be used to describe excessive weight include ***debu-debu*** and ***buyo-buyo,*** as in these examples:

Buchō no debu-debu shita musume wo yobandokō. Kanojo no shiri ni au isu wa nai kara. — Let's not invite the section chief's obese daughter. We don't have a chair that would fit her hips. (*O-debu no musume* is heard more often.)

Ano buyo-buyo bāsan wa anata ni te wo futte iru. — That flabby old woman is waving her hand at you.

That same ***buyo-buyo bāsan*** would be expected to have pendulous breasts, the word for which is ***tare-jichi*** (hanging breasts). Thus, if the circumstances indicate, she could also be called:

tare-jichi no oni-babā — devilish old woman with droopy tits

18

tare-jichi no hihi-babā-me — baboonlike old woman with saggy breasts

A flat-chested woman can be described as **pecha-pai,** the *pecha* coming from *pechanko ni naru,* "to be flattened":

Kare wa pecha-pai to kekkon shimashita. — He married a girl who has no tits at all.

Other germane expressions:

deppuri shita *(hito)* — dumpy (person)
toshima-butori — gain in weight that women may experience with the encroachment of middle age
zunguri shita *(hito)* — fat and short (person)
hyakkan debu — tub of lard (*Hyakkan* means 100 *kan* or 826 pounds.)
futotcho — blimp

In contrast to such heavyweights, we have the skinny ones. **Yaseru** is the verb meaning to lose weight, and from it derives **yase-koketa** (to be emaciated).

Sono yase-koketa otoko wa byōki ni chigai nai. — That emaciated man has to be sick.
Hisashiburi ni Yasube-san ni atta ga miru kage mo naku yasete imashita. — I met Yasube for the first time in a long while. He was a mere shadow of his former self (lit., so thin as not to even have a shadow).

19

Sō da yo. **Hone to kawa** *bakari sa.* — That's right. He's just skin and bones (lit., bones and hide).

Wags who wish to personalize this description can construct such names as:

Honekawa Sujiko — Miss Sujiko Honekawa (lit., Miss Sinewy Bonehide) This reminds me of how a friend once depicted such a woman. He said, "Putting your arms around her is like putting your arms around a sack of antlers."

Such ridicule can be extended to men by using this name:

Honekawa Sujio. (The final *o* indicates it is a male name, whereas a final *ko* signals a feminine name.)

There is a class of Buddhist ascetics who fast for religious purposes. Like Mahatma Ghandhi, these holy men usually do not have enough excess fat on them to feed a gnat for a day. They are called:

rakan — skin-and-bones Buddhist fanatics (The word was once applied to Buddha's five hundred disciples who had entered into the state of Nirvana.)

In the last extreme, those fleshless ones become mere:

ikeru shikabane — living corpses

Men who are not necessarily fat but whose bone

20

structure *(hone-gumi)* is huge can be disparaged with words like these:

udo — great awkward oaf
ō-otoko *sōmi ni chie ga mawari-kane* — The brain power of a big man does not extend throughout his body. (That is how the proverb translates but it's easier just to say, "You dumb lout.")

A David next to such a Goliath could be cut down with the following:

chinchikurin *na otoko* — dwarfish man
kobito — pygmy, runt, shrimp
issun-bōshi — Tom Thumb (lit., a one-inch monk)
Nani? Ore wa issun-bōshi datte? Kisama wa keshikaran kobito ja nai ka. — What? I'm a Tom Thumb? Why, you're nothing but an insolent runt, aren't you!

The Body and Physical Attributes

Face
nikibi-darake no kao — pimple-covered face
chimmurui no kao — face that would stop a clock
umeboshi-gao — prune face
minikui kao — ugly face
Yukiko no minikui kao wo mita dake de mushizu ga hashirimasu. — The mere sight of Yukiko's ugly face sends chills down my back.
Iinazuke no kao wo miru dake de Tomoe no muna-kuso ga

21

waruku natta. — The mere sight of her fiance's face nauseated Tomoe.

sukebege — lecherous face

Tarehoho no sukebege na tsuragamae datta. — It was a lecherous face with drooping jowls.

*Sanae wa me mo aterarenai kurai **hidoi kao** desu.* — Sanae's face is too awful to look at.

The following three words are all used to mean a stupid-looking face:

baka-zura
ahō-zura
manuke-zura

Eyes

yani-me *no oni-babā* — rheumy-eyed old devil of a woman

hingara-me *no baishō-fu* — cross-eyed prostitute (**Suga-me** means the same as *hingara-me.*)

de-me *no kōshokkan* — popeyed lecher

donguri-manako *no nozoki-mi* — goggle-eyed Peeping Tom (*donguri* is acorn; *manako* is another word for eyes).

kirenaga no me — slit-eyes

me no suri-agatta *Tōyō no onna* — slant-eyed Oriental woman

Ron–Pari no me — wall-eyes (lit., London–Paris eyes) Imagine that you are standing athwart the English Channel and are looking at both the cities simultaneously.

Mouth

***wani-guchi** no daigishi* — Diet member with the mouth of a crocodile

***ha-nuke** no samurai* — toothless samurai

deppa** no odoriko* — buck-toothed dancer (Soppa*** also means buck-toothed or, according to some sources, snaggle-toothed.)

Iki no kusaki wa nushi shirazu. — One is not aware of his own foul breath. (This is a literary expression used to describe someone who is blissfully unaware of his own faults. This is not, however, the case for the unfortunates around him.)

Nose

***kagi-bana** no saibankan* — hook-nosed judge

***tongari-bana** no bengo-nin* — lawyer with a pointed nose

***hanatare** kozō* — snot-nosed brat

Voice

***shagare-goe** no baka-busu* — hoarse-voiced, dim-witted, ugly woman

Forehead

***dekosuke** no suidōya* — beetle-browed plumber

Hair

***kebukai** kata* — hairy shoulders

***hage-atama** no suri* — bald pickpocket

ketō — hairy barbarian (usually meaning a Westerner)

Kanojo no oppai ni kowakute kuroi ke ga haete iru-tte. — I hear she has coarse black hairs growing out of her tits.

23

ke-darake *no momo* — hairy thighs
paipan — woman with no crotch hair

Legs
soto-ashi — knock-knees
soto-ashi no sambyaku-daigen — knock-kneed shyster
ganimata — bow-legged
ganimata no semmitsu-ya — bow-legged, dishonest real-estate agent (The Chinese characters for s*emmitsu-ya* mean "thousand-three-person." This vilifies real-estate agents who speak the truth only three times in a thousand.)

Odor

tsube-kuso-kusai — smelling of *tsube-kuso* (The word *tsube-kuso* covers a lot of ground. I have heard it used to refer to smegma, crotch cheese, toe jam, and dingleberries.)

Attire

buzama na minari — unsightly appearance
musakurushii minari — shabby attire

Ravages of Age

boke-*babā* — senile old strumpet

oni-*babā* — devilish old harpy, hell-hag
ha-nuke-*babā* — toothless old bat
samehada-*babā* — old woman with coarse-grained skin
   (lit., shark skin)
shiwakucha-*babā* — wrinkled old crone
oibore-*babā* — gross and aging hag
kusottare-*babā* — shitty old goat

Note: Substitute *jijii* for *babā* when referring to old men.

Just Plain Ugly

subeta — relentlessly ugly woman, gorgon
futame to mirarenai — shocking, hideous (lit., can't look
   at twice)
futame to mirarenai shūfu — hyena in skirts
busu — homely slattern
okachimenko — unsightly wench
bu-otoko — ugly brute
hyottoko — ugly person, gargoyle, distorted face mask
Anna hyottoko to kekkon suru nante tondemonai ze. — The
   thought of marrying such an ugly person is simply out of
   the question.
akujo — repulsive female

Miscellaneous

Japanese children have a chant that goes: *Okāsan debeso! Okāsan debeso!* Literally it means, "Your mother

25

has a protruding navel!" It is akin to, "Your mother wears flour-sack drawers (or surplus army boots)." It is not meant as a compliment.

This chant was popularized in 1965 by a comic group called Hana Hajime and the Crazy Cats. The full, somewhat incomprehensible chant ran:

Baka. Kaba. Chindon-ya.
Omae no kāchan debeso.
Omae no tōchan nana-iro debeso.
Mimi no ana kara te tsukkonde okuba
*   gata-gata iwasetaru de.*
Mendō mikirenē nā.

Fool. Hippo. Street musician.
Your mom's belly button sticks out.
Your dad's belly button has seven colors.
I'll stick a hand in your ear and rattle around
    your back teeth.
I just can't look after you.

TWO

Threats, Taunts, and Curses

Here is a prime selection of threats, curses, zingers, and rough commands as well as an ample supply of caustic words of chastisement, cautions, and sharp retorts.

I have given figurative translations (unless otherwise noted) since literal ones often fail to get the offensive ideas across. For instance: ***Sono te wa kuwan zo.*** — Literally this translates as, "I won't eat that hand." Since that doesn't really say much, I have elected to give readers a more figurative rendering. In this instance:

Sono te wa kuwan zo. — None of your bloody tricks now.

Threats

Needless to say, there are hundreds, even thousands of phrases and sentences that are used to intimidate others.

27

But since a complete list is out of the question, I have chosen a few as a starter kit:

Myō na ki wo okosu na. — Don't try anything funny.

Sunao ni naran to buchi-nomesu ze. — If you don't do what I say, I'm going to beat the hell out of you.

Shikaeshi suru zo. — I'll get even (for that).

Itai me ni awaseru ze! — You're going to feel it from me!

Hitotsu yaki wo irete yaru beki da. — I should teach you a lesson.

Mogaite mo shiyō ga nai. — It's no use struggling.

Aitsu yattsukete yaru. — I'll fix him.

Omote e dero. — Step outside.

Keri wo tsukeyō. — Let's settle this *or* Let's put an end to this. (The expression *keri wo tsukeru* comes from Japanese tanka and haiku poems, which often end with the auxiliary verb *keri*. Thus, "to add a *keri*" means to bring things to an end.)

Beso wo kaku yo. — You'll be sorry for this. (*Beso wo kaku* literally means to be on the verge of tears, to snivel and whimper.)

Ato de totchimete yaru ze. — I'll make you smart later.

Doteppara ni kaza-ana wo akeru kara oboete oke. — Remember, I'm going to drill a hole in your dirty guts. (This old expression was something used by swordsmen in the *chambara* movies, but it could also be said by a modern-day gangster pointing a pistol at a foe's stomach.)

Seibai wo shite kureru zo. — I'll destroy you.

28

Omae wo hakusei ni suru ze. — I'll have you stuffed and mounted.

Taunts

In Japanese the choice of pronoun for the speaker or the person spoken to can determine the degree of politeness or rudeness. *Ore,* for instance, is a haughty word for "I." Its use often suggests that you feel superior to the person you are addressing.

The man who uses *ore* is likely to use **omae** or **kisama** to mean "you." *Kisama* is a notch below *omae* in rudeness, so if you resent being addressed as *omae,* you should try this as a fiery retort:

Omae to wa nan da, kisama! — What the devil do you *(kisama)* mean by having the audacity to address me as *omae?*

Kisama nanka doko no dobu kara waitan da? — What sewer did you crawl out of?

Or if the other fellow persists in his rudeness, one could try:

Dare ni mono wo ii-agatterun da? — Just who the hell do you think you're talking to? (**Ii-agaru** means to speak up to someone. Its use makes it crystal-clear that you consider the person to whom you are talking to be far beneath you.)

Continuing the assault, one might say:

Namaiki ja nai ka. — You're damned impudent.

After that, this barb is flung at the wretch:

*Omae no taido wa **nattoran** ze.* — Your attitude is really
insufferable.

Finally, now that he's on his knees, he's finished off with:

Kisama no babā wo yatchaō. — Screw your mother.

And lastly, I want to note a toast popular during World
War II. For years I have treasured this little gem without
knowing just where I might ever make use of it. Once or
twice I was tempted to rise to my unsteady feet in a
Roppongi pub and shout it above the din of the revelers. I
didn't, but if I had, I wonder if those making merry carouse
would have cheered, thrown me out, or merely ignored me.
Probably they would have muttered *hen na gaijin* (strange
foreigner) in their *sakazuki* (saké cups) and looked away in
embarrassment. Anyway, here it is:

Shinshū fumetsu, kichiku Bei-Ei! — The Divine Land will
never die; down with the American and British fiends!

Familial Bliss

In Japan, it is said that the family that bathes together
stays together . . . with minimal discord. But now Japan
must gird its loincloth *(fundoshi wo shimeru)* and face up to

30

the harsh realities of *kokusai-ka* (internationalization). The day may soon come when the Japanese will have to endure their own adaptations of American-style soap operas and sit-coms:

SCENE: Eight-mat sitting room in a modest home in Adachi-ku, Tokyo
TIME: After the evening meal
ONSTAGE: A weary father, harried mother, and lustful daughter poised to go boy-hunting

DAUGHTER: *Otōsan, kuruma no kagi wa.* — Father, where are the car keys?
FATHER: *Aruite ike yo.* — You can walk.
DAUGHTER: *Sonna mucha wa iwan de ii.* — Cut the bull.
FATHER: *Nani. Kono komatchakureta hashita-me! Kuruma wo kashitara mata shōtotsu suru yaro.* — What? You cheeky wench! If I lend you the car, you'll just have another wreck.
DAUGHTER: *Shōtotsu. Nan no shōtotsu.* — Wreck? What wreck?
FATHER: *Tobokeru no wa yose.* — Don't play dumb with me.
DAUGHTER (aside to audience): *Kono toboke-oyaji-me.* — Old fool.

Enter Mother with next-door neighbor. Father has lurched to his feet and is looking around wild-eyed for a heavy, blunt object.

FATHER (shouting): *Kono zūzūshii surekkarashi ni*

31

namerarete tamaru mon ka! — I can't stand being made a fool of by this brazen hussy.

MOTHER: *Hito-sama no temae mo aru koto de wa arimasen ka. Mō yoshinasai, kono mikaikoku-jin.* — Don't you see we have company? Can't you aborigines cut it out?

DAUGHTER (to mother): *Yokei na tokoro ni kuchi wo dashite wa ikenai yo, kono hihi-babā-me.* — Butt out, you old baboon.

FATHER (livid with anger): *Nan datte. Kuchi no kiki-kata ni ki wo tsukero. Kono ama wa yakkai na shiromono ja nai ka.* — Wha-at? Watch your mouth. This little bitch has turned out to be an ugly customer to deal with, hasn't she?

DAUGHTER (flouncing out in a huff): *Bachi-atari jijii, kutabare!* — You can drop dead, you old fool!

Epithets

When one sees or hears someone involved in difficulties he deserves and has likely brought on himself, the warmth felt deep inside oneself can be expressed with the following expressions:

Zama miro. — It serves (him) right.

Zama miyāgare. — (This has the same meaning as the above expression but is even harsher in tone.)

Ii kimi da. — (same as above two) Note that this *kimi* is not the pronoun "you" but rather two separate characters meaning "sensation" or "feeling." Thus, "It gives me a good feeling to see him in that fix."

Nameru na. — Sez you (lit., Don't hold me lightly).

Dekei kao wo suru na. — Don't act uppity with me (lit., Don't make a big face). *Dekei* is rough for *dekai.*

Kuso! — Shit!

Kao wo aratte koi. — Wipe your nose (lit., Go wash your face).

Shomben de kao wo aratte koi. — (like the above but worse) Literally it means "Go wash your face with piss."

Te-yagande. — What the devil are you talking about?

Te-yande. — (ditto)

Nani itte yande. — (ditto)

Namakoku na. — Don't sass me.

Urusē. — Don't bug me! (Street patois for *Urusai!)*

Ussē. — (same as above)

Yogoreru is a verb meaning "to become dirty." Its stem **yogore** means "filth" or "dirt." Thus:

Kono yogore! — You scumbag!

In the same vein:

*Kono **o-kama.*** — You fag.
*Kono **hajisarashi-me.*** — You're a disgrace.
*Kono **baita-me.*** — You whore.

Abusing taxi drivers has long been a pastime in Japan, at least among foreign residents. I had my share of run-ins with this class, usually because they were surly, impolite, and reckless. At length, I had two cards printed in large quantities and always carried a supply with me, together with a small roll of Scotch tape.

Whenever I decided that the driver needed heated chastisement, I would tape one or the other of these cards on the back of the front seat, where all subsequent passengers could see it. (Both are quoted from *Japanese in Action* by the same author.)

One card read:

Jōkyaku no mina-sama: Saikin untenshu-busoku ni tsuki kokugo mo roku-roku hanasenai mugaku no kumosuke wo yatowazaru wo emasen. Igo taido wo aratamesasemasu kara kono tabi wa o-yurushi kudasaimase. Untenshu Torishimari-kyoku — To all passengers: Recently, because of the driver shortage, taxi companies have been forced to hire uneducated *kumosuke* who cannot even speak our national language correctly. Henceforth, we will see to it that they damned well change their attitude, so please bear with us this time. (signed) Driver Control Bureau

The other card read:

Jōkyaku no mina-sama: Saikin takushii-busoku ni tsuki arappoi unten sezaru wo emasen node go-jōsha no sai wa seimei hoken ni haitte kara o-negai itashimasu. Untenshu — To all passengers: Because of the present taxi shortage, we cannot avoid driving recklessly. Please be sure that your life insurance is up-to-date before you board this taxi. (Signed) Your driver

Your attention is invited to the word **kumosuke,** the

Chinese characters for which literally mean "cloud fellow." This term had its origins in the Edo period when it referred to palanquin bearers who transported people and luggage. These men often had no set abode and, like clouds, moved about looking for customers. Today it refers to a low-class driver of the kind described above: surly, rude, and guilty of *arappoi unten* (reckless driving).

When bandying libelous verbal abuse with such drivers, a potent barb would be:

Na-ani? Kumosuke no kuse ni. — What the? . . . Why, you're nothing but a low-class driver.

Rough Commands

When irritated with someone who persists in getting in the way, one can say:

Doita, doita! — Get out of the way! (The English translation is mild in tone, but in Japanese it's rough indeed. Even stronger is **Dokkyāgare!** or **Yokero!**)

In samurai times, feudal retainers would precede their *daimyō* shouting to peasants on the road:

Shita ni! Shita ni! — Bow down, bow down! (All Japanese have seen enough *chambara* movies to know the expression. This is not to be used unless you really want to rouse the ire of people in your path.)

Modern ways of telling anyone to disappear include:

Sassato userun da. — Get lost.

Doko ka itchae yo. — Get out of my sight.

Soko noke. — Move aside. (This is also a very rough expression, not something you should use with your mother-in-law, no matter how sorely tempted.)

Totto to kaere! — Get out!

Use the following as circumstances dictate:

Shikujiru na. — Don't screw it up.

Katte na netsu wo fukun ja nai. — None of your damned impudence.

Tsubekobe wo iu na, kono zubekō. — Enough of your complaints, you wench.

Yokei na o-sekkai da. — None of your blasted business.

Ōki na o-sewa da. — None of your bloody business.

Jibun no atama no hae wo oe. — Mind your damned business (lit., Chase the flies off your own head).

Ore ni oyabun-kaze wo fukasete mo hajimaran zo. — Don't play the big shot with me.

Mono-ii ni ki wo tsukero. — Watch your tongue.

Now we lower our standards a little:

He de mo kurae. — You just try it (lit., Eat my fart).

Kuso kurae. — Eat shit.

If you hear such phrases, you can say:

Gesu-batta koto wo iu na. — Don't talk dirty.

36

Curses

We begin with definitions:

norou — to curse
nonoshiru — to verbally abuse
akutai wo tsuku — to use abusive language
akkō suru — to revile
noroi wo kakeru — to place a curse on

Three fundamental curses all meaning basically the same are:

Chikushō! — Damn (you)! *or* Curses (on you)!
Kuso!
Ima-imashii!

These words can be used in a general sense (Damn it all) or specifically (Damn you). They are puzzling inasmuch as the basic meaning of each differs. As we will see in the chapter on animal-related insults, *chikushō* actually means "beast" while *kuso* is "shit" and *ima-imashii* is an adjective meaning "vexing" or "irritating." Nonetheless, all are used to convey the same thing.

"Drop dead" is translated directly into Japanese as **Shinde shimae** (lit., Die and be done with it). You can also say *Shinyāgare*, which could be given as "Die in the presence of a superior," namely, the speaker.

Kutabare. — Drop dead *or* Curse you.
Kutabatte shimae. — Drop dead.

A rather strange curse:

Kuso shite shine! — Shit and then die!
Kuso shite nero. — Shit and go to sleep (I confess that I see little connection between death, defecation, and deep slumber).

Other potent curses are:

Bachi de mo ataryāgare. — The devil take you (him/her) *or* Go to hell. (*Bachi* or *batsu* is "punishment from God," and *ataru* is "to befall or strike." Thus, "May punishment strike you.")
Kono bachi-atari-me! — (Although this has the same meaning as the preceding expression, you could never figure it out from the grammar. The sentence literally translates as "this punishment-befallen fellow.")
Kōtō yūmin mina bachi ataryāgare! — Curse the idle rich!

Other such expressions:

Katte ni shiro. — Do whatever you please and be damned.
Berammē! — Damn you, you bloody fool!

The following expression is used in utter exasperation with someone who is being simply too ridiculous for words:

Tōfu no kado ni atama wo butsukete shinde shimae. — Drop dead! (lit., Hit your head on a corner of tofu and die).

38

When I first heard this curse long ago, I understood correctly the first word to be *tōfu* (soybean curd), but I shook my head in doubt and thought, No, that can't be. How could anyone die from hitting his head on the corner of a piece of *tōfu?* Maybe it's *tōku no kado* (a far-off corner). At least, that would make more sense than *tōfu no kado.* So I misused the expression for a year or two, lending fuel to my growing reputation as a *hen na gaijin* (an oddball foreigner). At last I got it right, but I still wonder how one can die from striking his head against bean curd.

THREE

Use of Living Creatures as Tools of Defamation

Reptiles and Amphibians

There is still lurking in man's subconscious a hostility toward many living creatures. This hostility began when we were not the dominant species on this planet but survived only as frightened nomads in flight from savage four-legged hunters.

Even after the roles were reversed and we became the savage hunters, the old mind-sets—practically instincts—remained, and we continued to distrust and dislike animals. (Hence the hunters' philosophy: If it moves, shoot it!)

To rationalize our instinctive animosity, we attributed to animals unsavory characteristics that were either undeserved or deserved to a lesser degree than popularly believed. We did this also to justify our callous slaughter of other species—to stave off or alleviate our guilt-plagued nightmares. Even in words like nightmare (a female horse that torments us in the night) we can detect this animosity toward animals.

It is likely that most or even all races denigrate other homo sapiens through offensive comparison with animals, fowl, fish, and even insects. In learning Japanese insults based on such comparisons, however, the reader should bear in mind that the characteristics he or she attributes to other species may not be the same as those the Japanese assign to them. Even when the characteristics are the same, there may be a question of degree.

A handy example is the snake. Aside from herpetologists, most Westerners abhor snakes and shudder at their sight. Possibly this hostility harks back in large part to the biblical snake (actually, Satan disguised) which first tempted Eve to sin in the Garden of Paradise. The Japanese have no such myth, which is not to say, however, that they love snakes.

Additionally, in the U.S. at least, there are far more dangerous snakes and in larger numbers than in Japan. The *mamushi* and the *habu* are Japan's only *dokuja* (poisonous snakes) and except on the pleasant southern isles of Amami, they have never intruded largely into the popular consciousness. Americans, on the other hand, have long been harassed—or so we like to believe—by rattlesnakes, water moccasins, copperheads, and coral snakes. Doubtless, the harm inflicted and the danger presented by these scaly crawlers have been exaggerated (most reptiles, with the exception of the king cobra, fear man as much as we fear them), but we have long belittled people and places we despise through reptilian simile and metaphor; a snake in

41

the grass, the snake pit, cherish a snake in the bosom, and so forth.

But, in Japanese, to compare a person to a snake doesn't carry that much punch, although *Kare wa hebi da* (He's a snake) does suggest a certain degree of cunning.

Aside from that, the only instances that come to mind concern the *uwabami* (translated as both boa constrictor and python) and *dakatsu* (snakes and scorpions):

uwabami no yō ni nomu — to drink like a fish (lit., like a python)

Yūbe uwabami no yō ni o-sake wo nonda kara, kyō wa futsukayoi de nyūin saseraremasu. — I am being hospitalized today with a hangover, because I drank like a fish last night.

Dakatsu no yō ni kirawarete imasu. — (He) is despised (lit., hated like snakes and scorpions).

Another reptile that can be used to vilify is the turtle or *kame*, particularly if one says **dongame** (dull turtle):

Omae no yō na dongame wo yatou to wa yume ni mo omowan zo. — I wouldn't dream of hiring a dull turtle like you.

Then there is **deba-game** (turtle with buckteeth), which means "a Peeping Tom":

Sono otoko wa deba-game da to wakattara imōto wa zekkō shita. — My younger sister broke off with that fellow when she learned he was a Peeping Tom.

Marine Life

Shifting to the finny creatures and their co-dwellers of the deep, let's examine the large variety of comparative disparagements we can find among them. First, the whale:

geiin suru — to drink like a whale
Ojiisan wa maiban Roppongi atari de geiin shimasu. — Grandfather swills it down every night in Roppongi or thereabouts.

Same is a word for shark (*fuka* is another), and ***same-hada*** describes rough, coarse skin:

tonari no okusan no same-hada — the coarse skin of the wife next-door

Sometimes we see old farming women whose backs are permanently rounded from long years of bending over in the rice paddies. Their backs must have reminded someone of the curved backs of prawns (*kuruma-ebi*):

kuruma-ebi babā — old hunch-backed woman

Detarame is a rather mystifying insult, for its literal translation is "protruding cod eyes," but its actual meaning is "nonsense." The *de* is from *deru*, "to come out," while *tara* is "cod" and *me* is "eye."
Detarame wo iu na. — Don't talk nonsense *or* Tell that to the horse marines.

43

Kingyo means goldfish, while *deme-kin* is the so-called telescope-eye goldfish, a variety with popeyes. From this word is constructed:

deme-kin no bakayarō — popeyed fool

Very large mouths remind some of alligators, thus the expression:

wani-guchi — person with a very large mouth (lit., alligator mouth)
wani-guchi no onna — woman with a large mouth

A *kappa* is a mythical river monster that appears in stories for children:

He no kappa *sa.* — It's nothing (lit., It's just a river monster passing wind). This describes something of no value or significance.

The **tengu** is another mythical creature, described as a long-nosed goblin. The *tengu* is also said to be extremely arrogant, a trait which has given rise to the following expressions:

Shiranakatta ka. Kare wa **fuda-tsuki no tengu** *da.* — Didn't you know? He's a world-class braggart. (*Fuda-tsuki* means to have a label attached.)
tengu no yori-ai — assembly of braggarts
tengu-banashi — boastful story

Kanojo ni iwasetara koibito wa Nihon-ichi no kanemochi da. Tengu-banashi kashira. — To hear her tell it, her lover is the richest man in Japan. I wonder if she's just bragging.

sukan-tako — disgusting fellow (lit., a disliked octopus)

Ano yō na sukan-tako no soba ni iru to ge ga desō da. — Just being beside him makes my gorge rise.

Rats, Rabbits, and Weasels

Nezumi is a rat or mouse, while **dobu-nezumi** is a gutter rat. A person's morals can be traduced with the use of this scurrilous construction:

dobu-nezumi no dōtoku — morals of a gutter rat

Another rather puzzling reference to *nezumi* is:

atama no kuroi nezumi — dishonest servant (lit., a black-headed rat) Is there such a thing as a rat with a black head and body of a different color? Or does the black refer to the color of Japanese hair?

A rabbit-related insult that sprang into the public cognition not long ago was **usagi-goya,** or "rabbit hutch":

Nihonjin wa usagi-goya ni sunde iru to iwaremashita. — The Japanese were said to live in rabbit hutches.

If you dislike the way your dinner companion keeps

staring at you with black, beady, unblinking eyes, you might say:

Itachi no yō na me *de mitsumeru na.* — Stop staring at me with those beady eyes.

Still another puzzling expression (not really an insult) is:

itachi no michi-giri wo suru — to cut off relations with someone (lit., to cut the path of a weasel)

Insects

Mushi is the everyday term for insects (or bugs) while the scholarly term is *konchū*. *Kemushi* is a caterpillar and gives us example of how two cultures view the same object differently. I don't know that many of us would care to cuddle a caterpiller but we certainly don't hold the degree of hostility toward them that the Japanese do. I have heard, however, of one variety of Japanese caterpillar that stings, which may be a contributing factor:

kemushi no yō na yatsu — despicable fellow (lit., some-one like a caterpillar)

Other insect-related taunts are:

yowa-mushi — weakling (lit., weak bug)
hehiri-mushi — small brat (lit., farting insect)

46

mushi-kera — scum
tentori-mushi — bookworm (lit., a grade-taking bug)
naki-mushi — crybaby
gokiburi teishu — a lazy, good-for-nothing husband
(*Gokiburi* means cockroach.)

Fowl

The only offensive remark with feathers on it that comes to mind is ***washi-bana*** or eagle nose:

Sensei, watakushi no washi-bana wo naosu shujutsu wa arimasen ka. — Doctor, isn't there an operation to fix my eagle nose?

Four-legged Creatures

This is an area that produces much perjorative vocabulary. The modifier ***yotsu-ashi no*** (four-legged) is sure to wound. And there are others:

yotsu-ashi no yabanjin — bestial barbarian
*Kono **chikushō-me!*** — You beast!
Konchikushō-me! — You brute!
*Sono **kedamono-me!*** — That animal!
Sonna kōdō wa chikushō no asamashii shirushi da. — Such behavior is the mark of the beast.
yajū — a savage beast; a beastly person
Sono hanzai-nin wa yajū no yō na mon da. — That criminal is a beast.

47

Dogs and Monkeys

The Japanese equivalent of the expression "fight like cats and dogs" is "fight like dogs and monkeys."

Ano futari wa itsumo **inu to saru no yō ni** *kenka wo shite imasu.* — That pair is always at it like cats and dogs.

Although dogs (*inu*) may be man's best friends, they get their share of verbal knocks in Japan:

keisatsu no inu — a police spy
Kono **inu-me!** — You dog!
inu no tō-boe — useless complaining (lit., the barking of a far-away dog) It refers to a weak person or coward who speaks badly of others behind their backs, without ever coming out and saying what's on his or her mind. Thus, it's like a dog barking at a person or a strong opponent from a safe distance.
inu-goroshi — dogcatcher (lit., dog-killer) To compare a person to a dogcatcher is sure to get his attention and raise his hackles.
inu-zamurai — depraved samurai
inu-boneori — fruitless efforts (lit., dog-bone-breaking)
inu-tsukubai — fawning (lit., dog-crouching)

Westerners tend to think of members of the monkey family as clever, agile, and rather amusing creatures. Although perhaps some Japanese feel similarly, the

48

following three expressions indicate the general feeling is otherwise:

saru-mane-ya — copycat (lit., someone who imitates things like a monkey)
yamazaru — hillbilly (lit., mountain monkey)
Ano gunsō wa saru da. — That sergeant is a cunning, crafty fellow (lit., He's a monkey).

A **hihi** is a dog-faced baboon. By adding *jijii* (old man) or *babā* (old woman), we get two very sharp barbs:

hihi-jijii — dirty old man, lustful old goat, horny geezer (lit., baboonlike old man)
hihi-babā — lewd old woman (lit., baboonlike old woman)

Badgers

The badger *(tanuki)* is considered in Japan to be a crafty, rather amusing creature with supernatural powers. It is used in such gibes as:

tanuki-jijii — cunning old man
tanuki-babā — crafty old woman
furu-danuki-me — sly old fox

Foxes

Like the badger, the fox *(kitsune)* is regarded as a wily, crafty, though not so amusing animal:

49

kitsune no yō na kodomo — foxy child

Rural Japanese also assigned mystical powers to the fox:

Wakai toki ni sono hyakushō wa kitsune ni tsukareta sō desu. Ima de mo nan to naku okashii yō da. — It is said that farmer was possessed by a fox when he was young. Even now there's something strange about him.

Cows

As a field to plow for derisive commentary, cows offer little and can almost be ignored, except for two examples:

ushi no yodare no yō — unending, something that drags on (lit., like a cow's saliva)
Bokushi no sekkyō wa ushi no yodare no yō deshita. — The preacher's sermon seemed like it would go on forever.
ushi-pai — heavy breasts (The *pai* comes from *oppai* or breasts.)
Kanojo no ushi-pai wa honmono deshō ka. — Are her huge breasts real?

Cats

In most cultures, except perhaps that of ancient Egypt, and to a lesser degree, present-day England, *neko* (house cats) have often received short shrift. Japan is no exception.

neko wo kaburu — to pretend to be innocent, to be hypocritical (lit., to put on the cat).

neko ni koban — to cast pearls before swine (lit., gold coins to cats)

neko-baba — embezzlement (lit., feline feces) This comes from felines' habit of covering up their business with dirt when they're finished.

neko no me no yō ni kawari-yasui — extremely fickle (lit., changeable as a cat's eyes)

neko-pai — flat-chested (lit., cat tits) Can you imagine any girl so poorly endowed?

Although it is not really an insult, *neko* is a diminutive colloquialism used to refer to those ladies of the arts called geisha. *Neko wo ireru* (bring in a cat) means to call in a geisha. Possibly this originated in the use of catgut for the strings of the shamisen geisha often strummed.

Other Felines

If I go out and get sozzled, you can use this expression to describe me:

tora ni naru — to get blind drunk (lit., to become a tiger)

If the gendarmes collar me, they may take me to a *tora-bako,* or drunk tank (lit., tiger box). Such "tigers" can be divided into two groups — the big and the small:

ōdora — drunkards (lit., big tigers)

51

kodora — drinkers (lit., little tigers)

Shishi is an odd word with many meanings, but we are interested here in the one that means "lion":

shishi shinchū no mushi — treacherous friend (lit., an insect in a lion's breast) Although I unfortunately have had frequent opportunity to make use of this phrase, it is not very common. You may find that only Japanese of a literary bent will know it.

shishi-bana *or* ***shishippana*** — broad, flattish nose

An insult for which one would be long remembered:

Sono hito ni atte hoshiin datte. Tondemonai! Sono yō na shishi-bana no kebukai yabanjin wa dai kirai. — You want me to meet him? Out of the question! I despise that flat-nosed, hairy barbarian.

If you have visited Okinawa, you may recall seeing ***kara-shishi*** there. These statues of "lion-dogs," mythical creatures with horrendous faces, usually stand guard in front of temples and tombs. They are called China lions in English.

Buchō no okusan no kao wo mita kai. Kara-shishi wa ii toko da. — Did you see the face of the section-chief's wife? Even a China lion's face would be an improvement.

kara-shishi babā — old woman with a face like a China lion

52

Pigs

Despite a reportedly rather high level of intelligence, the reputation of the pig suffers from its appearance and perhaps from noisy table manners.

*Sono **buta** no yō na daimyō wa Mito-han no shishi ni ansatsu saremashita.* — That swinish daimyo was assassinated by patriots of the Mito clan. (This *shishi* is written with different *kanji* than the word for lion.)
tonji — my son (lit., pig-child)
tonsai — my wife (lit., pig-wife)
*Kono **buta-yarō!*** — You pig! (lit., this pig-guy)

Bears

A freak show in a Japanese circus might display a ***kuma-musume,*** a "bear-girl," or a girl with hair over most of her body.

dango-bana no kuma-musume — hairy girl with a dumpling nose
Hayaku okiru toki shujin wa kuma mitai yo. — My husband is like a bear when he gets up early. (The Japanese connotations are the same as the English.)

Horses

Let's look at a sampling of how the Japanese compare horses with people. One reading for the character for horse is *uma* and another is *ba*.

yaji-uma — curious rabble (lit., jeering horses)

tsuke-uma wo hiku — to be followed home by a bill-collector (lit., to lead a trailing horse)

doko no uma no hone da ka wakaranai otoko — man of doubtful origins, a drifter (lit., horse bones from nobody knows where)

iki-uma no me wo nuku yō na otoko — a shrewd, very cunning man (lit., a fellow who can steal the eyes out of a living horse)

uma no ashi — poor actor (lit., a horse's leg)

uma no mimi ni nembutsu — water off a duck's back (lit., a prayer in a horse's ear)

baji tōfū — unheeded words (lit., an easterly wind in a horse's ears).

baka — fool (lit., a horse-deer)

gyūin bashoku suru — to swill and gorge (lit., to drink like a cow and eat like a horse)

umazura — horse-face

jaja-uma — shrew, virago, termagant (lit., restive horse)

*Oyaji to **uma ga aimasen**.* — I don't get along with my old man (lit., Our horses don't match). This need not be insulting, but usually when you don't get along with someone, it is implied that you don't like his words or actions.

Dinosaurs

TV movies for Japanese children have made such creatures as Godzilla widely known. The names for these grotesque monsters often end in -*gon*. Someone added -*gon* to a word for mother and came up with:

54

Mama-gon — a forever-scolding hell-hag of a mother

Monsters, Beasts, and Fiends

Here are some items of virulent vocabulary that malign brutes, devils, and inhuman scoundrels:

Kono akuma-me. — You devil.
akuratsu na — cruel and unscrupulous
hitode-nashi — monster
Kono hitode-nashi me! — (You) brute!
nimpinin — a brute in human shape
chikushō otoko-me — (same as above)
hakujō na gokudō-me — heartless and debauched brute
gokudō yarō — monstrous villain

Similar words and their usage:

hannya no mōshigo — demon-child
Uchi no musume wa umareta toki ni sugoku kawaii tenshi da to omotte yorokonda ga ima ni nattara hannya no mōshigo da to wakatte iru. — When our daughter was born, I thought she was a cute little angel, but now I know that she is a demon-child sent by Satan.
giri mo ninjō mo shiranai gokudō-mono — man devoid of all sense of duty and humanity
Sono onna to wakareta ato kanojo wa giri mo ninjō mo shiranai gokudō-mono to issho ni natta. Zama miyāgare. — After that woman and I parted, she took up with a man devoid of any sense of duty and humanity. It serves her right.

ningen no kawa wo kabutta konchikushō — an animal in the form of a man

Ojōsan ni ii-nasai yo. Hitori de kōchō-shitsu ni hairanai hō ga ii. Ano otoko wa ningen no kawa wo kabutta kon-chikushō da kara. — Tell your daughter that she shouldn't go into the principal's office alone, because he's an animal in the form of man.

bakemono — a spook

Sono akiya ni bakemono ga iru to iu no ka. Omae wa sono yō na hanashi wo shinjiru noroma ka. — You say there are spooks in that vacant house? Are you such a bonehead as to believe that story?

Four

Sex, Booze, and Money

Sex, Immorality, and Marital Relations

The Japanese take a fairly lenient view of sexual indiscretions, but even so there are limits, and people can be quite clear in denouncing excesses.

Yūjirō wa mainichi te wo komanuite midara na mōsō ni fukette iru yō da ga nani mo jitsugen shinai kara betsu ni fūki wo midashimasen. — With folded arms Yujiro spends his days lost in lascivious thoughts, but none of his fantasies materialize, so he does no special harm to public morality.

Judging from the frequency in which they are mentioned in literature, Japan has its share of lusty men (*seiyoku no tsuyoi* otoko-tachi). They are described in such words as:

sukebei — lecher; lecherous
sukebei-oni — lecherous devil, world-class womanizer
inran na otoko — satyr
shikima — sex fiend
injū — lascivious beast, filthy fiend
nikuyoku no gonge — incarnation of carnal desire

Sukebei is the most often heard of these words, and women may use it when a man tells even a mildly racy joke. It is heard so often that some foreign students mistakenly take it to mean something akin to, "You naughty rascal, you!"

I heard a story (I believe it is not apocryphal) of an eager young American who was sent to join his company's branch in Tokyo. Being a hustler and something of a wag, he had learned a little Japanese to employ in cocktail-party repartee. Laboriously, without the aid of a teacher, he managed to string together a few words in Japanese that he imagined to be equivalent to the English, "Hey, you sly old dog! Getting any new stuff these days?"

Thus far, so good, and at the next martini testimonial given by the gigantic Japanese corporation, which was tied up with the American's company in some commercial arrangement, he sighted the august Mr. Sakimura, the widely respected chairman of the board. Throwing caution to the winds, the young American sashayed up to this forbidding presence and said clearly, *Oi, Sakimura-san, dai-ichi sukebei hanchō-san ja nai ka.*

Mr. Sakimura gasped, blanched, and spun on his heels, for the young American had said something like "Hey there, Sakimura, if it isn't just the biggest lecher of them all."

58

Not long after that, the hapless American was sent home without even the courtesy of a sayonara party.

Bottom line: Don't use *sukebei* to or about anyone unless you really mean to say he is a lecher . . . and not merely a playful old rascal!

I have heard lewd women with whom I consorted say *sukebei-gami* (lecherous paper) to identify the tissue they used to wipe away the aftermath of a sexual encounter. It may be that they use this word more to foreigners than to their fellow countrymen, since *sukebei* was a word that ninety-nine percent of all American G.I.s in Japan knew and spoke with marked frequency. *Sakura-gami* (cherry paper), on the other hand, was a highly absorbent paper that Japanese women, lewd or not, used to ward off pregnancy.

Japan's **mizu-shōbai** ("water business" or nightlife world) has always been fascinating, especially the demimonde. My first direct experience came shortly after World War II in the town of Hachioji. My two red-blooded comrades and I, on our first night, had found our way unerringly to what we called in my native Texas, with charming delicacy, a good-time house.

For nearly three years before that we had been studying the Japanese language and culture from nisei and kibei teachers. These instructors had filled our eager ears with stories about the marvels of Japan's **karyū-kai** (flower-and-willow world), so we had salivated lustily awaiting this night.

Even the terminology bespoke the wonders to which we would be treated. Flower-and-willow world, indeed! And those who toiled among the flowers and willows were called by such names as **baishumpu** (a woman who sells spring) and ***baishō-fu*** (a woman who sells laughter). Even the establishment where they awaited us horizontal on their workbenches was called a ***baishun-yado*** (inn that sells spring). Less fancy nomenclature includes:

akasen chiiki — red-light district (lit., red-line area)
kōtō no chimata — gay quarters
imbai-yado — brothel, cat house
jorō-ya — whorehouse, sporting house

Anyway, it would have been more fitting if our teachers had taught us yet another word for the business of prostitution, namely, ***doromizu kagyō.*** Its meaning, "muddy-water profession," would have been far more appropriate to the dirty, plain girls with runny noses who were paraded before us that evening just before we fled into the night.

A Southern gentleman once greeted his guest, who was just descending from a train, with the words, "Wal suh, shall we indulge in a mint julep first or proceed direct to the hoah house?" In similar spirit, you might ask your Japanese guest for the evening:

*Sā, ippai nomō ka. Sore tomo **yūjo-machi ni chokusetsu ikō ka.** — Well, shall we have a drink? Or should we go directly to the district of playful women?*

Women who deal in spring are also called those who "play" *(asobu)*. Another reading of the character for *asobu* is *yū*, which gives us the following three words for a red-light district:

yūjo-machi
yūri
yūkaku

Other such vocabulary items are:

iro-zato — gay quarters (lit., color-village)
iro-machi — gay quarters (lit., color-town)
fuyajō — gay quarters (lit., castle of no night)
girō — brothel

Reminiscent of mothers who called Hell "the bad place," a few Japanese of Victorian bent referred to those areas that market springtime *(haru wo hisagu)* as:

yokunai tokoro — bad place
yokaranu basho — (same as above but slightly more literary in tone)

The managers and pimps go by a variety of names, *pombiki* and *ponchan* being the basic two. Also, we have:

himo
genji-ya
gyūtarō

The business of dealing in human flesh (what in the West is called white slavery) is *jinshin baibai,* while a person engaging in this sordid trade is a *hito-kaiya* (lit., person-buyer) or a fleshmonger. *Yarite-babā* can be used to mean a procuress.

61

Women who sell their bodies *(mi wo uru)* can be called any of the following, which all basically mean prostitute. The following first four terms specifically refer to a streetwalker:

shūgyōfu
gaishō
yotaka — (lit., night hawk)
tsujigimi
jorō
pampan
pansuke
oyama
baita
baijo
imbai
machi no onna — (lit., woman of the town)
yami no onna — (lit., woman of the darkness)

Some of these terms of defamation can be quite flowery. For instance:

machi no tenshi — (lit., angel of the town)
yami no hana — (lit., flower of the darkness)
tsukimi-sō — (lit., primrose)

Or they can be crudely direct, such as:

doya-pan — flophouse slut
shōgi — licensed prostitute
Nido to sono doya-pan wo kono uchi ni irenai kara oboete

oke. — Just remember, I'm never again letting that flophouse slut in this house.

Loose women who have not quite crossed the line into professionalism are given such names as:

inran na onna — lewd woman
bakuren onna — abandoned woman, gutter trull
ikagawashii onna — woman of ill repute
daraku onna — woman of uncertain reputation (I could never really understand what was uncertain or dubious about the reputation of these women. After all, a whore is a whore.)
shiri-guse no warui onna — woman who sleeps around (lit., a woman with bad hip habits)
shiri ga karui onna or **shiri-garu onna** — (same as above) Literally, a woman with light hips that are easily moved from *futon* to *futon*.
ama — slut, bitch
fūgi no warui onna — demi-rep, hooker
hasuppa musume — wanton girl

An apprentice geisha is a **maiko** (alas, a dying breed). When she becomes a full-fledged geisha *(ippon ni naru),* she loses her virginity to a high-bidding customer in a ceremony called **mizuage-shiki.** *Mizuage* means to land fish or to lift fish from the water. The connection between hoisting a netload of fish onto land and the defloration of a *maiko* is not clear. Perhaps it is better that way.

In any event, the geisha (some prefer the word *geiko*) may

thereafter change bed partners often or may remain faithful to one patron for many years. She may even take a lover (students are prime candidates) on whom she lavishes gifts and gelt. Whatever form her *futon* fun takes, however, the true geisha is not usually thought of as a whore, although some do sink to that level. Such are called:

korobi-geisha — (roll-over geisha)
imosuke — (potato gal)
daruma-geisha — (lit., round-bottomed geisha) This term comes from the *daruma* doll, which rolls over easily but always regains a vertical position.
sanryū-geisha — (third-class geisha)
shomben-geisha — (piss geisha)
haori-geisha — geisha wearing a *haori* coat (A true geisha would never wear a *haori.)*

During periods of hostility and armed tension, girls called *ian-fu* (girls with no elastic in their drawers) were dispatched to combat areas to comfort the boys. Most of this comforting was carried on silently in a horizontal position.

An older term for chippy that one may still come across is *keisei,* as in the proverb:

Keisei ni makoto nashi. — There is no truth in the words of a whore.

At one time in Japan's colorful past, a species of doxy must have loitered in or around the public bathhouses *(sentō).* These bathhouse prostitutes were called *yuna,* and thereby hangs a tale.

When then President Ronald Reagan visited Japan and addressed the Diet, he essayed a short sentence in Japanese. My guess is that he intended to say, *Nichibei no yūkō wa eien desu,* or "Japanese-American friendship is forever."

I was listening to the speech on satellite television with several native speakers of Japanese, including the incumbent Mrs. Seward, who thought that what Reagan had said in his poorly enunciated Japanese was, *Nichibei no yuna wa taihen desu,* which would have meant something like, "Japanese-American bathhouse prostitutes are a real handful."

My wife, being of a literal turn of mind, immediately sang out, "I wonder how he found that out so quickly. He's only been in Japan two days."

Less direct ways of referring to those of wonderously easy virtue whom the French call *filles de joie* (women of joy) are:

ichiya-zuma — (wife for one night)
ichi-nichi koibito — (sweetheart for a day)

Pamma is a tart who doubles as a masseuse. Once, years ago, an American friend stayed in a hotel with the telltale sign of the *sakasa-kurage,* upside-down jellyfish, outside. Getting settled in, he asked the front desk to send up a masseuse. Signals must have gotten mixed, because when the woman arrived, it soon became apparent that the service the American wanted was not the one the woman

65

intended to provide. To the woman's exasperation my friend kept insisting that she rub him down, so finally she drew herself up proudly and announced in ringing tones, "Me no masseuse. Me whore!"

Another word with the same meaning as the above *pamma* is ***nadekko-san,*** whose provenance is complicated. *Naderu* is the verb for "to stroke, fondle, or caress," and from the same character comes *nadeshiko*—a flower called a pink. The name of this flower is also used in the expression *Yamato nadeshiko,* or a "traditional daughter of Japan." Since a *Yamato nadeshiko-san* is at the other end of the social scale from a *nadekko-san*, it must have been somewhat of a cynic who dreamed it up.

Sometimes a distinction must be made between a hooker who serves Japanese men and one who spreads joy among Westerners. ***Wapan*** is the former, and ***yōpan*** and ***yōshō*** are both names for the latter.

While not a prostitute, of course, a Japanese woman who lives with a Westerner is called an ***onri,*** or "only" ("I speak true. You are only one").

Let me interrupt this rather lengthy listing of Japanese words for prostitute to remind the reader that there is also a cornucopia of such terms of disparagement in English: trollop, fallen woman, floozie, slut, trull, hustler, drab, hooker, bin, ten-penny slut, call-girl, street walker, bawd, doxy, lady of the evening, demirep. I have even heard such women referred to as "Mrs. Warren."

Moving up in the professional world, we encounter the corresponding expressions for the higher-class prostitute:

puro no onna (This means a woman of the profession,

while a *hai-puro,* or "high-pro" is a high-class bestower of joyful laughter.)

From days past come three words meaning prostitute that are rooted in Japanese culture:

shiro-kubi — (lit., white-neck; from the powdered necks and low nape-lines of dancers, serving girls, and geisha)
shira-byōshi — (This comes from the term for the promiscuous dancing girls who performed in traveling troupes and kept up the rhythm of the music with white clappers called *hyōshi.)*
bikuni — (The primary dictionary definition is a Buddhist priestess but a secondary meaning from the Edo period is a low-class prostitute dressed as a nun. Further inquiries, however, reveal there was a time in Japanese history when Buddhist nuns of a certain sect roamed the countryside begging alms for their home-temple and offering sexual favors to the hesitant as a persuasive device. Mnemonic: a *bikuni* in a bikini).

Rashamen is another word from the past that is nonetheless familiar to most Japanese. It means "a foreigner's mistress," and the charm of the word lies in its origin. *Rasha* is a kind of wool cloth, and *men* is short for *menyō,* or "sheep." This wool cloth was imported into Japan by some resident Westerners (perhaps Dutchmen), and, in time, the people of Nagasaki began to nickname Westerners *rasha.*

Then some people chanced to look into the bedrooms of these *rasha,* where much to their amazement, sheep appeared to be asleep on several of the beds . . . with Western men. Always ready to believe any outlandish story about the hairy barbarians, the natives concluded that the Westerners had an excessive fondness for barnyard creatures and were keeping ewes for fun and erotic relaxation. Such sheep were called *rasha no menyō* (a foreigner's sheep), which came to be shortened to *rashamen*.

At last, the Japanese got a closer look into those bedrooms and discovered to their dismay that what they had fondly imagined to be sheep were nothing more than large dogs sleeping at their masters' feet. By then, however, the word *rashamen* was already in use, so when Japanese women replaced the dogs in foreign beds, the derisive appellation transferred to them.

In Japan, honest lust is one thing, while perversion *(hentai seiyoku)* is quite another. Deviates are usually described with the adjective *etchi na,* which approximates the *h* sound in *hentai seiyoku*. A rank degenerate could also be called a *henshitsu-sha.*

A classic usage of the terms was seen in 1936 in the murder trial of the infamous Miss Sada Abe. Sada and her lover had been shacked up for several days in an inn in Tokyo's Arakawa Ward. There they had engaged in a sex marathon that shocked even the hardened maids of that "hot pillow" inn. Being a *rinki-onna* (jealous woman), Sada hated the thought of her paramour returning to the arms of his wife when their tryst ended. She did not want to share him (or his equipment) with anyone, so while he was asleep she cut off the poor devil's unit with a kitchen knife, after which he bled to death. To cap her hard night's work,

Sada carved a line of *kanji* on Kichizo's thigh. It read, *Sada Kichi futari,* "Sada and Kichi, the two of us."

At her trial, the prosecution considered charging Miss Sada with being a **hentai seiyoku-sha** (sexual pervert) but at last relented and changed the wording of the charge to **ijō seiyoku-sha** (an oversexed person). Sada smilingly admitted to the latter term—it was the former that had outraged her. "Sexual pervert, indeed!"

One night, I chanced to enter a restaurant and found a Japanese acquaintance of mine quarreling with a woman who turned out to be his mistress. He saw me and asked that I join them at their table. He then introduced the woman as *Yarase no Michiko desu.* This broke me up, for *yaraseru* is the verb for "to let do." Meaning? "This is Michiko who lets anyone do it with her."

When a Japanese husband starts to openly engage in extramarital exploits, he is said to be a **fuda-tsuki no uwaki-mono,** or "infamous womanizer" (lit., philanderer with a label attached). Thereupon, the man's wife may begin to burn with jealousy and can be said to be a **yakimochi-yaki,** or "grilled rice cakes." Rice cakes *(mochi)* are heated *(yaku)* in the hottest flames of a charcoal fire. It is the intensity of these flames that is likened to the passion of jealousy.

If a woman's complaints drive her husband to desperate measures, he may become a **gokudō teishu** (rotten, filthy brute) and his wife may refer to him in such scathing words as **uchi no gokudō** (my brute *or* the brute of our house). She might also call him **uchi no nora** (my stray).

On the other hand, if the wife has become the domineering one in the family, **kakā denka** (petticoat government) can be said to be the form of administration governing their domestic lives. She will have become a *kampaku nyōbō* (bossy wife), and he a *nyōbō kōkō no teishu* (a uxorious husband).

Tanabe-san no uchi wa kakā denka da yo. Kare wa itsumo nyōbō no shiri ni shikarete iru kara . . . — Mr. Tanabe is a hen-pecked husband; he is always at his wife's beck and call (lit., spread out like a cushion under his wife's hips).

To continue the tale of Tanabe:

Tanabe-san takes to strong drink and gets swacked as often as he can afford. With his *nomi-nakama* (saloon cronies), he frequents a ginmill called the Bar Madrid. The first night he and his *daraku-nakama* (fellow profligates) went there, the Mama-san (bar manageress) asked their names. Tanabe introduced each of the four as:

Yopparai-san — Mr. Drunkard
Nondakure-san — Mr. Sot
Yoidore-san — Mr. Toper
Hidari-kiki-san — Mr. Lush

Mama-san laughed and asked Tanabe-san's name. In unison, the four cried, *Hidari-uchiwa-san!*

Literally, *hidari-uchiwa* means "left fan" or, by slight extension, a fan that is held in the left hand. The expression can also refer to a man who enjoys a good, idle life while living off the earnings of his daughter or wife.

70

In this case, Mrs. Tanabe was a hard-working teacher, while her *sodai-gomi* (outsized garbage) of a husband seemed to be forever unemployed.

Why a fan held in the left hand? To keep the right hand free to pour and drink saké, of course.

Later, Mrs. Tanabe calls the Bar Madrid and talks to Mama-san:

TANABE: *Tanabe desu ga, uchi no sodai-gomi wa guden-guden ni yotte iru deshō ka.* — Is my pile of garbage there and is he already snockered?

MAMA-SAN: *Jitsu wa.* — Well, the truth is . . .

TANABE (her voice has become strident): *Sō omotta wa. Sate, sono dōraku-mono wo denwa ni yonde kudasai.* — I thought as much. Well, call that libertine to the phone.

MAMA-SAN: *Chotto muzukashii desu ga. Yuka no ue de yoitsuburete imasu kara.* — That may be a little hard to do. He's passed out on the floor.

Money

It is called *okane* as well as: **kinsen, tsūka, shihei, kahei, genkin.** Those of us who hate to part with even a small amount of it are called:

nigiri-ya — tight-fisted person
gametsui hito — miser
shimittare — tightwad
ichimon-oshimi — skinflint
rinshoku-jijii — scrooge

71

Uchi no danna wa totemo kane-banare ga warui wa yo. —
My husband is very close-fisted.
Kotchi no wa motto yo. Sukoburu-tsuki no kechimbō desu.
— Mine is worse. He is a notorious penny pincher.

Stinginess is related to greed *(yokubari)*. Relevant expressions are:

don-yoku — (same as above)
Kimi no don-yoku wa taishita mon da. — Your greed really
overwhelms me.
yokubari-babā — greedy old woman
haikinshū-shugi — worship of money (or the god
Mammon)
shusendo — money-grubber

Those of the opposite persuasion (like my irresponsible daughter) toss their money to the winds like grain. They are called *rōhisha* or spendthrifts.

Uchi no musume wa yumizu no yō ni okane wo tsukaimasu.
Tomeyō to suru to kanojo wa tonkyō na himei wo ageru.
— My daughter spends money like water. When I try to
stop her, she utters a hysterical scream. *(Yumizu means
hot and cold water; tonkyō is hysterical.)*

Sooner or later the spendthrifts fall heir to *kinketsu-byō*
(lit., shortage-of-money sickness). They become:

monnashi — deadbeats
okera — penniless persons

They begin to bum off *(takaru)* their friends. If it is my wanton daughter, she may come home as a shin-gnawer *(sune-kajiri)* and sponge off her old man. When I see her, I think:

Shakkin ga kimono wo kite aruite iru yō na mon da. — She is like borrowed money walking around with a kimono on.

She'll tell me spitefully:

Otōsan wa kechi-kechi shite iru kara sugu soko no shichiya ni itte okane wo kariru wa. — Because you're such a skinflint, I'll just go to that pawn shop down the street and borrow some money.

And I'll reply:

Ano iji-kitanai jijii ka. Yoshita hō ga ii zo. Kare wa moji-dōri no kyūketsuki da. — That swinish old man? You'd better give up that idea. He's a veritable bloodsucker.

FIVE

Mind and Mouth

Voices and Words

Voices may be soft and soothing, or they may grate on your nerves.

kare-goe — hoarse voice
shagare-goe — grating, raucous voice

It may be a shrill voice, or *kiiroi koe* (lit., a yellow voice), or one that is offensive to the ears *(mimi-zawari)*.

Sono mimi-zawari na koe wa mō iya da. — I just can't stand that rasping voice anymore.

As in English, a nasal voice *(hana ni kakatta koe)* is one that whines:

Saburō wa asa kara hana ni kakatta koe de nakigoto wo itte iru. — Saburo starts with his whining complaints in the morning. *(Nakigoto,* "crying things," are complaints.)

A ***gami-gami*** *onna* is a shrew while a *gami-gami babā* is an old shrew. To be especially merciless we can add the verb *hoeru* (to bark):

Uchi ni kaettara kami-san wa sugu gami-gami hoe-dashita. — As soon as I got home, my old lady started her noisy fault-finding (*Hoe-dasu* means to start barking).

When a person's words make no sense at all, we can characterize them by saying:

gu ni mo tsukan *koto* — terrible nonsense, absolute tommyrot
chōkō-zetsu — long-windedness (The characters stand for long, wide tongue.)
Nakasone-san no chōkō-zetsu ni aki-aki shite shimaimashita. — I grew tired of listening to Mr. Nakasone's long-windedness.
Kare no gu ni mo tsukan kurigoto wa zenzen suji ga tōtte imasen. — His ridiculous ramblings make no sense at all.

Three withering sentences to effectively blacken someone's ability in Japanese are:

Taitei no Amerika no gaikōkan wa nihongo no ni no ji mo shirimasen. — Most American diplomats do not know word one of Japanese (lit., don't even know the *kanji* for the *ni* in *nihongo*).

hana-mochi naranai — intolerable; detestable (lit., the nose can't bear it)

Karera no nihongo wa hana-mochi narimasen. — Their Japanese stinks.

*Karera no nihongo wa **tende sama ni narimasen.*** — Their Japanese is lousy.

When we focus on English, we find:

Eigo no ei no ji mo shiranai. — (He) doesn't know any English at all.

susamajii *eigo* — terrible English

shafu eigo — pidgin English, kitchen English (This is an older expression. *Shafu* means rickshaw puller. Rickshaw pullers spoke neither refined nor correct English, if they spoke any at all.)

A port jargon called the Yokohama dialect could be heard in the 1860s and 1870s. Its practitioners said *Walk allimasu* for *Wakarimasu* (I understand), among other depravities. These deficients also used expressions like the following:

coots pon pon — bootmaker (*Kutsu* are shoes or boots and *pon pon* is bang bang.)

okee aboneye pon pon — big dangerous earthquake (*Okee*

76

is *ōkii,* or "big"; *aboneye* is *abunai,* or "dangerous"; and *pon pon* is "bang bang" for "earthquake.")

Japanese who learned enough English to become fairly adequate interpreters and translators were often looked down upon by other Japanese, who called them *eigo-zukai,* or "English-users." This name seems harmless enough in English, but in Japanese it is definitely pejorative.

Broken English can be expressed as *katakoto-majiri no eigo,* as in:

Ra Mōru no mama-san ga boku no kao wo miru nari katakoto-majiri no susamajii eigo wo hanashi-hajimeru.
— As soon as the Mama-san at the bar Rat Mort sees my face, she starts speaking in terribly broken English.

If a person's *kanji* and *kana* are written in a slovenly hand, we may call him or her a *sho ga mazui hito.* Such words are quite hurtful in Japan, where people take much pride in the quality of their handwriting. *(Sho* is the *on* reading for the character meaning to write.)

Mental Capacity

The Japanese have been fairly inventive in devising words that cast shadows on the function and the contents of minds. There are so many ways to say that someone is a meathead or half-wit that I can list only the more common here. Unless otherwise noted, they all carry the clear message that the person under fire is a knucklehead and maybe even chicken-witted to boot:

tonchiki-me — (lit., dull and foolish in spirit)
Kono tonchiki-me yarō! Totto-to dete ike! — Get out of here, you fool!
hiru-andon — (lit., a day-time night lamp; in other words, someone as stupid as a lamp that burns in the bright of day)
tōhenboku-me — (lit., a Chinese-changing stick.) The etymology is unclear.
wakarazu-ya — thick-headed person
Kono kyōshitsu ni wakarazu-ya bakari ga iru node sensei wa hara wo kiru tokoro da. — Because there is nothing but dolts in this classroom, the teacher is about to commit hara-kiri.
ahō — dumb ass (This is as often heard as *baka* but has a somewhat gentler sound.)
manuke — dimwit (lit., out of place)
gubutsu — foolish chucklehead
usunoro — feeble-witted
tawake-mono — dunce *(Tawakeru* is a verb meaning to talk foolishly while *mono* is "person.")
nō-nashi — brainless
Ano nō-nashi to kekkon shita no ga somo-somo no machigai da wa to iinagara obasan wa naite imashita. — Sobbing, my aunt said that her first mistake was to have married such a know-nothing.
baka — fool
ō-baka — great fool
noroma — dummy

anpontan — simpleton

Kono anpontan-me! Hira-shain no bunzai de namaiki ja nai ka. — You simpleton! You're impertinent for a mere clerk.

o-medetai — scatterbrain *(Medetai* by itself means congratulatory but with the prefix *o-* it means someone not playing with a full deck of cards.)

Omae no kareshi wa o-medetai yatsu bakari da. — Your boyfriends are all morons.

tansai-bō — guy who is short on talent

tomma — (lit., a dull horse)

kabocha-me — cabbage head (lit., pumpkin head)

The word *baka* can be intensified with precedents like these:

origami-tsuki no baka — acknowledged fool

shōshin shōmei no baka — downright fool

sokonuke no baka — out-and-out fool (lit., bottomless fool)

akireta baka — hopeless dingbat

kamaboko-baka — (lit., fish-cake fool; a fool pinned to a board like a fish cake)

tanjun-baka — simple nitwit

usura-baka — trifle wanting in the brain department, dumbshit

o-baka Santarō — big dolt Santaro (like the television character)

All of the following also accuse the target being disparaged of stupidity:

gūtara — addlepated loafer
gujin — ninny
oroka-mono — harebrained
bonyari-mono — absent-minded person
Sono bonyari-mono no Saburō wa mata kuru no wo wasureta. — That absent-minded Saburo has forgotten to come again.
nukesaku — bonehead (lit., with the makings left out)
toroi yatsu — sluggish dolt
shiremono — dunderhead
yotarō — ignoramus (*Yota* is nonsense and *rō* is fellow.)
ahondara — yo-yo (This word probably comes from *ahodara-kyō,* a parody on a Buddhist sutra.)
Seijika wa mina yoku ga fukai ahondara de komaru. — It is frustrating that the politicians are all greedy yo-yos.
nō-tarin — short on brains
o-hitoyoshi — naive simpleton
o-tenten — feather-brained *(Tenten* is the word to describe something floating around like a feather.)
o-tsumu-tenten — (essentially the same meaning as above. *O-tsumu* is a children's word for head.)
boya-boya shita hito — absent-minded goose
Sono boya-boya shita hisho wo hayaku kubi ni shinai to akaji ga deru yo. — If you don't fire that absent-minded secretary soon, we'll go into the red.

You may come across these as well:

toppoi yatsu — someone a little weird in the head, cuckoo
Nihon onchi — someone who knows nothing at all about Japan

sempaku chishiki — superficial knowledge
nameru — to make a fool of
mono-oboe ga noroi — to be slow-witted, a slow learner
chinō shisū ga hikui — to be of low mentality, a nitwit
donkan na baita — stupid whore
atama ga usui — dumb (lit., thin head)
Kono do-ahō. — You dunce.
nō-miso ga kusatta hito — person with rotten brains, ignoramus

The following illustrate usage:

Tawakeru na. — Stop playing the fool.
Yabo na koto wo kiite wa ikan. — Don't ask me stupid questions.
gariben suru — to plug away
Sono seinen wa gariben de aru no ni igai ni gigochinai bunshō wo kakun da. — Although that youth is very industrious (at school), he writes very awkward sentences.
shō-gakkō chūtai — grade-school dropout
hana-hojikuri-me — nose-picker
Namaiki ja nai ka. Kono shō-gakkō chūtai no hana-hojikuri-me ga. — You are very impudent for a nose-picking grade-school dropout!
yoppodo no noroma — nincompoop, dummy
Kimi wa yoppodo no noroma da nā. — You really are quite a nincompoop, you know.
baka-banashi — drivel
Omae no baka-banashi wa mō takusan da. — I've had enough of your drivel.

81

kokoroe-chigai — misguided
baka na baita — ignorant slut
Jein omae wa kokoroe-chigai no baka na baita da. — Jane,
  you're a misguided, ignorant slut.
*Jiten de baka to iu kotoba wo hiite mireba omae no shashin
  ga notte iru.* — If you look up the word *baka* in a dictionary, you'll find your photograph there.

Sometimes the origins of these words of execration will
help to lodge them more firmly in your memory:

keikōtō — slow to catch on (lit., a fluorescent lamp)
tempo-sen — simpleton (lit., a coin of the Tempo era
  [1830–33] not worth even a *sen* today in actual mon-
  etary value)
sukotari — lacking a little upstairs (*suko* from *sukoshi*,
  "little," and *tari* from *tarinai*, "to be lacking")

Beyond simple stupidity lies actual pathological mentality and even insanity. **Kichigai** is the most common
word for insane. Also:

machi no hakuchi — town idiot
ki ga furete iru — simple simon, addlepated
hidari-maki — (Perhaps "eccentric" is closer to the true
  meaning, literally, "wound left.")
teinōji — idiot child
kurukuru-pā — touched in the head (This was popularized
  by Mr. Tony Tani, a TV comedian of the 1960s.)
Matsuzawa-yuki — looney (This refers to an old Tokyo
  institution well-known for both its rose garden and its

resident lunatics. The expression means you are on your
way to the Matsuzawa Psychiatric Hospital, and not as a
visitor.)

*Kono **kichigai-me!*** — You moron!

*Kono **hakkyō-me!*** — You imbecile!

boke — befuddled

Nihon-boke — befuddled mental condition that comes
from long residence in Japan

As pointed out elsewhere, a great many words in
Japanese cannot be translated into English precisely. To
enjoy their full favor, we must rely on figurative instead of
literal interpretations. ***Berammē*** is such a word:

berammē kotoba wo tsukau — to use rough, vulgar speech
(most often refers to the speech of gangsters and other
flotsam of the streets of Tokyo)

Characteristics of *berammē* speech are the substitution
of *e* for *a* and the rolled *r*. Instead of *Yatsu no bero wa
shiroku-nai ja nai ka* (Can't you see that his tongue is not
white?), an Asakusa pimp would be more likely to say,
Yatsu no berro wa shiroku-nei ja nei ka.

Closely related, in sound at least, to *berammē* is ***berabō,***
which means "terrible."

berabō na hito-de — an awful lot of people

berabō ni isogu — to be in a terrible hurry

Berabō-me! — Confound it!

Nani wo iu no ka kono berabō-me — I'll see you in hell.

SIX

Origin, Status, and Employment

Origins

In Japanese society, much attention is paid to where you come from and what your role *(hombun)* is. Because origin and position are so important, they are often referred to when belittling others. This is sometimes accomplished through the speaker's choice of pronouns, verbs, and verb endings, the choice of which will show respect or contempt, or denigration is achieved by the judicious use of words of debasement.

Take the words identifying provincial people as examples. Such words clearly reflect the dichotomy between city and rural cultures. Americans, for example, have always poked fun at rural folk, calling them hayseeds or hillbillies. It is acknowledged, nonetheless, that lives of culture and sophistication may be led away from the metropolitan turmoil and clamor. Persons of wealth and refinement do occasionally seek out the quieter and more sedate existence vouchsafed by the countryside.

Not so in Japan. If a city *bunka-jin* (man of culture) does retire to the hinterlands, it is only in search of affordable housing in which to spend his declining years.

True, there are many **inaka no narikin** (rural nouveaux riches) these days who are using their new land-based wealth to travel abroad and acquire samples of the beaux-arts. In the fullness of time, this may ameliorate the contempt with which rustics are viewed, but that day has not yet dawned. Regard how disdain for the country dwellers is manifested in words:

inakappe — country oaf
inaka-kusai — backward (lit., stinking of the country)
yamadashi — yokel (lit., out from the hills)
akagetto — plowboy

The term *akagetto* is particularly interesting when you consider its literal meaning, "red blanket." At some time in Japan, red blankets must have been widely sold and used for warmth by the country people as they walked along the roads in winter. So much so that *akagetto* became a synonym for a country oaf or hayseed.

Tsuchi-gumo is defined as a contemptible country bumpkin. The literal meaning is "earth-spider," the word for a race of subhuman cave dwellers of early Japan.

Then there is **o-nobori-san,** or "honorable-climbing-person." The honorifics *-o* and *-san* are, of course, cynically meant, while *nobori* suggests that the rural lout must rise from the uncultured depths whenever he is presumptuous enough to intrude in the rarified atmosphere of the capital.

Tagosaku also means clodhopper while ***nōkyō-san*** is a more modern term deriving from the abbreviation for *Nōgyō Kyōdō Kumiai,* or the "Federation of Agricultural Cooperative Associations." This federation arranged domestic and foreign tours for its members (mostly farmers), and the sight of these bright-eyed, camera-packing groups led by flag-carrying guides was a common one. Such tourists are meant by the term *nōkyō-san.*

In Tokyo slang, we have the merciless construction ***dasai-onna.*** The following exchange illustrates the expression's origin:

A: *Kichizaemon no okusan ni aimashita ka. Hidoi wa yo.*
— Did you meet Kichizaemon's wife? She's really awful.

B: *Naze?* — Why?

A: *Naze ka to iu to reigi-sahō wo shiranai otemba-san dakara yo.* — Because she's a boisterous minx who doesn't have any manners.

B: *Datte, Saitama-ken desu mono.* — But she's from Saitama (Prefecture), isn't she?

So to get *dasai-onna* we take the *da* of *datte* and the *sai* of *Saitama,* thus showing the contempt some of the fancy folk of Tokyo have for their country cousins from Saitama to the north.

The most scornful of all such expressions may well be ***yamazaru,*** or "mountain monkey"; the most common is the milder ***inaka-mono,*** or "country person."

ki no kikanai inaka-mono — dull-witted hick
Sonna ki no kikan inaka-mono ni kiite mo muda da. — It
   won't do any good to ask a dull clodhopper like that.

Two names often found among unlettered menial girls of
low class are *Mii-chan* and *Hā-chan*. To call someone by
these names indicates the low level of that person's tastes.

Mii-chan Hā-chan muki *no eiga* — a low-brow movie
   (lit., suited for Mii-chan, Hā-chan types)
Mii-chan Hā-chan muki no shōsetsu — a low-brow novel

The male equivalents of the above are *Hassan, Kuma-san*
(from *Hachikō, Kumakō*) and are used in the same way.

Other expressions contemptuous of low-brows include:

doro-kusai *hashita-me* — uncouth wench *(Doro-kusai*
   means smelling of mud.)
atsukamashii *surekkarashi* — brazen hussy
nari-agari *onna no kuzu* — trashy upstart of a woman
zubutoi *hashita-me* — cheeky wench
*Ani wa nari-agari onna to kekkon shita kara chichi ni
   kandō sareta.* — Because my elder brother married a
   worthless upstart of a woman, he was disowned by our
   father.

Hombun (One's Role in Society)

Persons of little account can be traduced with virulent
expressions like these:

87

gomi-tame yarō — scumbag
chimpira-me zako — pick-nose, small fry
*Karera wa **tada no zako** ni suginai.* — They're nothing more than small fry.
shōjin — Another word for small fry (lit., small person)
*Kono **kusottare!*** — You shitty little creep!
*Kono **iya na gaki-me.*** — You odious brat.
minohodo wo shiranai — to not know one's place
Tonari no hara-guroi hehiri-babā wa minohodo shirazu da. — That crafty old fart next door does not know her place.

By now the reader may have noticed that *kono* (this) coupled with a noun of contempt, and *me* (fellow, guy, wretch) is one formula for a direct insult. *Me* is the Chinese character's *on* reading and *yatsu* is the *kun* reading. The spoken *yatsu* is usually masculine, the *me* is quite as often feminine, as we have seen in other examples. In any event, "You so-and-so!" is most readily expressed by this formula: *Kono* — (so-and-so) — *me!*

Employment

Censure is often achieved by referring to how people earn their daily rice. In the entertainment field, we find:

daikon yakusha — poor actor (lit., giant radish actor)
joyū kuzure — wreck of an actress, has-been actress
danyū kuzure — wreck of an actor

jari tarento — television actor or actress who appears only a few times and then disappears from the scene forever

(The likes of *jari-tarento* infest Japanese television in such large numbers that I suspect that the oft-heard rumor is true — that the show producers promise to put these young hopefuls on television just to work their lusty wills on them, after which they give them the *hiji-deppō,* or "cold shoulder" (lit., elbow rifle). *Jari* literally means gravel. *Ko-jari* (small gravel) is used to mean street urchins, and *tarento* from the English "talent" has been adopted into Japanese to signify personality, as in a television personality, not special abilities.

Hearty maledicta can be heaped on writers in these three ways:

kakedashi no sammon bunshi — amateur hack writer
heppoko bunshi — penny-a-liner
kōshoku bungaku no kakedashi no sakka — fledgling writer of pornographic literature

Doubts are cast on the qualifications of men of medicine with the word **yabu-isha,** which means an ignorant doctor or quack:

Yabu-isha no kureta kusuri wo nondara obasan ga sugu ni nakunarimashita. — My aunt died immediately after taking the quack's medicine.
Ano otoko wa isha-tte? Tohō mo nai hanashi da. Yabu-isha no shikaku mo nai. Ena-gaisha no shain dake da.

89

— That man a doctor? That's absurd. He's not even a quack. He's just an employee of an afterbirth disposal firm.

Hebo-isha also means quack. In fact, *hebo* preceeding any occupation raises doubts about qualifications:

hebo-bunshi — writer of little skill
hebo-ekaki or *hebo-gaka* — dauber
hebo-shijin — poetaster
hebo-shokunin — bungling workman
hebo-yakunin — an incompetent official
yakunin no hashikkure — a government official of low rank.
Are? Tada no yakunin no hashikkure da ze. Fuku-daijin no kaban-mochi da. — Him? He's just a low-ranking government official. He's no more than a briefcase carrier for the vice-minister.

Similar in meaning and usage to *hebo* (and *yabu*) is *pē-pē,* as in these examples:

pē-pē yakunin — a petty official
pē-pē yakusha — inferior actor
pē-pē-zumō — low-ranking sumo wrestler
Sono pē-pē yakusha wa itsumo me-ue no hito ni peko-peko shite iru. — That inferior actor is always bowing and scraping to those above him.

Beginners at any gainful activity could be called *zubu no shirōto,* or "rank amateurs."

At the bottom of the job-respect scale are:

bataya — rag-picker
suigara-hiroi — snipe shooters, those who pick up cigarette butts

Persons with no visible means of support, bums, vagrants, or tramps, include:

fūraibō — tramp
furōsha — vagrant
horōsha — bum
fūten — a young vagrant, juvenile delinquent
furō no to — street scum
Uchi no mei wa furōsha to shite omawari-san ni ageraremashita. Hashi ni mo bō ni mo kakaranai yatsu da. — My niece was picked up by a policeman for vagrancy. We haven't a prayer that she will ever be worth a fig. (*Hashi ni mo bō ni mo kakaranai* literally means "can't even be snagged with [something as small and thin as] a chopstick or [as big and wide as] a stick.")

SEVEN

Repugnant Personal Traits (Ad Hominem Insults)

Most of us at one time or another are guilty of exhibiting undesirable behavior. Admitting to it, however, does not mean it can be forgiven or forgotten. In this chapter we will see with what impassioned invective the Japanese describe those deserving of such censure.

Vanity and Arrogance

In a vertical society like Japan's, it is expected that people will play the game of butter up and trample down, with the tramplers taking on the colors of arrogance. What is puzzling to the Westerner, however, is that arrogance assumes the guise of paternalism and is widely accepted. On the other hand, vanity arising from appearance or possessions is frowned upon.

nobosete eragaru — to be swollen with vanity

*Jimbō-kun wa mada ketsu ga aoin da ga nobosete eragatte
iru.* — Jimbo has little experience, but his head is
swollen with vanity.

unuboreru — to be vain; be conceited; have a high opinion
of oneself

*Kare no okusan wa jibun de wa zessei no bijin da to
unuborete imasu.* — His wife fancies herself to be a
peerless beauty. (*Zessei no bijin* is a world-class
beauty.)

Selfish, Cold, and Cruel

The following behavior, although exhibited by most
peoples, is not so pronounced in Japan, where people
display a good amount of consideration *(omoiyari)*.

wagamama no gonge — living embodiment of selfishness
ingō jijii — cruel old man, scrooge
hana-tsumami-mono — a heartless rat, a mean skunk (lit.,
a person or thing to hold one's nose at)

*Aitsu to kekkon shite wa ikan yo. Chi mo namida mo nai
hana-tsumami-mono da.* — Don't marry him. He's a
heartless rat. (*Chi mo namida mo nai* means to have no
blood or tears.)

reiketsu-kan — cold-blooded villain

*Otōsan wa itsumo sono yō na koto wo iu wa. Mae no ii-
nazuke wa kangae no hinekureta reiketsu-kan da to ittan
ja nai ka.* — Dad, you always say something like that.
You said my last fiance was a cold-blooded villain with
a deranged mind.

wagamama no daimeishi — synonym for a selfish lout

Sono joyū no namae wa wagamama no daimeishi to narimashita. — The name of that actress has become synonymous with selfishness.

Grumbling

Complaining within the bosom of one's family was permitted in feudal Japan, but grumbling away from home—especially in the presence of superiors—was not to be tolerated.

*Kono **yakamashiya**.* — You grumbler.
***guchippoi** kijirushi* — bellyaching weirdo

Gluttony

Those who are slaves to their bellies are condemned with these words, all meaning glutton:

ō-gurai
kuishimbō
taishokuka or **bōshokuka**
Kono bōshokuka wa wagaya no tsura-yogoshi da. Uma hodo kuun da. — This glutton is a disgrace to our family. He eats like a horse.

Manners

Reigi and *reigi-sahō* are basic words for manners. ***Reigi wo shiranai*** means not to know one's manners. Other vocabulary in this context includes:

shitsuke ga warui *kodomo* — ill-mannered child
bushitsuke *na yarō* — rude fellow
soya na kotoba-zukai — rude language
yabo *na otoko* — boorish man
futekusare-me — sulky, ill-mannered wench
shitsurei — impolite
burei — rude
doro-kusai — uncouth (lit., stinking of mud)
no-sodachi — born in a barn (lit., raised in a field)
Ima no hanashi no doro-kusai sonchō wa no-sodachi darō.
    — The uncouth village chief we were talking about was
    probably born in a barn.
jakyō-to — heathen
gōman burei — haughty and rude
Mukashi sono kuni ni itte ita senkyōshi wa itsumo butsu-
    butsu itte imashita. Gōman burei na jakyō-to ni
    kakomarate iru kara fuyukai to no koto da. — The
    missionary who went to that country long ago was
    always complaining. He'd say how unpleasant it was to
    be surrounded by haughty and rude heathens.
ha ga uku — to set one's teeth on edge, be repulsive (lit.,
    one's teeth float)
Ano gunsō wa ha ga uku yō na gendō wo suru otoko desu.
    — That sergeant is a man of repulsive and nauseating
    behavior (lit., he's enough to set one's teeth afloat).

Stubbornness

Stubborn refusal to abide by the dictates of society and
government in feudal Japan often brought harsh punishment
to the recalcitrant.

ganko ittenbari — obstinacy itself
Shichō wa giron-gamashikute sono ue ganko ittenbari da.
   — The mayor is argumentative as well as extremely
   stubborn.
gō-tsukubari — a headstrong person; a diehard
Kono gō-tsukubari-me. — You stubborn and unyielding
   fellow.

Lies, Exaggeration, and Slander

Uso is the most common word for "lie" and judging
from the frequency with which it is heard, you would think
that Japanese spend their days immersed in prevarication.
This impression is aided by the multitudes of girls and
young women whose every third word it seems is *"Uso!"*
which they employ much like the English "You don't say!"

mie-sugita uso — obvious lie
shira-jirashii uso — barefaced lie
hora-fuki no uso-tsuki — boastful liar
gongo dōdan na uso-tsuki — outrageous liar
hora — big talk, hot air *(Hora* is also the word for a
   trumpet shell.)
hora wo fuku — talk big, boast
hora-fuki or ***ōbora-fuki*** — braggart, boaster; bull-shitter
hora-banashi — exaggerated story
dokuzetsu-ka — person with a spiteful tongue
chūshō suru — slander, fling dirt at a person's reputation
*Kono shūkanshi ni wa Gō-san wa fuketsu na dokuzetsu-ka
   da to kaite arimasu.* — In this weekly magazine it is
   written that Mr. Go is a filthy man with a poison tongue.

Kanojo wa shiriai wo minna chūshō suru kuse ga aru. —
She has the habit of slandering all her acquaintances.
Godaiin-san wa ōbora-fuki de hyōban desu. — Mr. Godaiin
has the reputation of being a well-known liar.

Cowards and Sissies

Cowards are despised as much in Japan as elsewhere,
but sissies, though looked down upon, do not receive as
much opprobrium as in the West.

The first five words of the following fundamental
vocabulary all mean coward:

okubyō-mono — coward
koshinuke
hikyō-mono
shōshin-mono
funuke
memeshii otoko — sissy
yowamushi — wimp
niyaketa otoko — pantywaist
ikareponchi — namby-pamby

The Japanese have at least two ways of making
reference to a man who is bold and fearless (maybe even
domineering) at home but mild-mannered and shy when
facing the outside world, that is, a lion at home and a mouse
abroad:

uchi-Benkei or *kage-Benkei* — a tiger at home (Benkei
was a historical personage.)

ikuji-nashi — gutless sissy

chiisai ketsu no ana — cowardice (lit., small anus)

Kono ikuji-nashi no ketsu no ana wa donna ni chiisai deshō ka. — What a chicken-hearted coward this fellow must be (lit., I wonder how small this wimp's asshole is).

yowaimono-ijime — bully

okubyō — cowardice

Sono yowaimono-ijime suru koshi-nuke no na wa okubyō no daimeishi to narimashita. — That bully's name has come to stand for cowardice.

niyaketa — namby-pamby

Kono goro Tōkyō ni niyaketa gaijin no otoko ga ōi, ne. — There are a lot of namby-pamby foreign men in Tokyo these days, aren't there?

Wrongdoing

It goes without saying that among a law-abiding people like the Japanese, those who violate laws are held in deep disdain indeed. And although even members of organized criminal gangs have a certain moral code of their own, they do not rate much higher in public esteem. Some basic words:

hannin — criminal

zainin — criminal

dorobō — thief

nusubito — thief

nusutto — thief

kosodoro — sneak thief

petenshi — con man

98

pakuri-ya — swindler

gorotsuki — hooligan, hood

yota-mono — a hooligan, rowdy

Aitsu wa keshikaran yota-mono da. — He is a damned hoodlum.

chō-honnin — ringleader

Sono akumei-dakai chō-honnin wa mada tsukamatte imasen. — That infamous ringleader still has not been caught.

jōshū-han — habitual criminal

Arabu sekai de wa mambiki no jōshū-han no te wo kiri-hanashimasu. — In the Arab world they cut off the hands of habitual shoplifters.

akudama — bad guy, villain (lit., a bad ball)

Seibugeki no akudama wa dōshite itsumo kuroi bōshi wo kabutte iru no kashira. — I wonder why the bad guys in Western movies always wear black hats.

Slang words that are equivalent to pilfer or filch are:

choromakasu

kusuneru

kapparau

Sune ni kizu wo motsu literally means to have a scar on the shin, but figuratively means to have a shady past:

Zada-kun wa dōmo kusain da. Sune ni kizu wo motte irun ja nai kashira. — Zada really looks suspicious. I wonder if he doesn't have a shady past?

All sorts of crimes and criminals:

chijō ni yoru hanzai — a crime of blind passion
Furansu de wa chijō ni yoru hanzai no shobatsu wa wariai ni karui. — In France the punishment for a crime of passion is relatively light.
burai no shōnen — juvenile delinquents
machi no shirami — the criminal element (colloquial, lit., town lice)
Sono burai no shōnen wa jiki ni machi no shirami ni naru to omou. — I think those juvenile delinquents will eventually turn into gangsters.
kusai meshi wo kuu — to serve time in prison (lit., to eat smelly rice)
Yoshi-nasai. Tsukamattara omae wa nagai aida kusai meshi wo kuu darō. — You'd better not do it. If you're caught, you'll be in prison for a long time.
baba-korogashi — swindling old women
jiji-korogashi — swindling old men
Dōkyūsei no Wada-kun wa sagi-shi de baba-korogashi semmon da. — My classmate Wada turned into a crook and specializes in swindling old women.

Inchiki is a handy and often-used word that means false, fraudulent, phoney, or fake:
inchiki shōbai — monkey business
inchiki-gusuri — quack medicine
inchiki-gaisha — bogus company
inchiki kabuya — fraudulent stockbroker

More crookedness:

ikasama — false, crooked

100

Mata nanika ikasama wo yaru no ka. — Are you going to do something crooked again?

Lazy, No-Good So-and-So's

As industrious a race as the Japanese are, there are nonetheless those among them who pass their hours in idleness and contribute little to the betterment of themselves or others. They are described with the following:

namake-mono — lazy fellow
norakura-mono — lazy fellow
guzu — sluggard
yaku-tatazu — good-for-nothing
goku-tsubushi — good-for-nothing
dame-otoko — no-good man
dame-onna — no-good woman
doku ni mo kusuri ni mo naran — of no redeeming value (lit., can't become either medicine or poison)
roku-de-nashi — a good-for-nothing, a worthless fellow
kuso no yaku ni mo tatanai — worthless (lit., can't even be used for shit)

A: *Kono yō na roku-de-nashi na yatsu wa kuso no yaku ni mo tatanai. Uchi-kubi ni shitara ikaga deshō ka.* — This rascal is not worth a shit. How would it be if I decapitated him?

B: *Kawaisō to omowanai ka.* — Wouldn't you feel sorry for him?

A: *Zenzen. Datte doku ni mo kusuri ni mo naranai shiri-omo ja nai ka.* — Not in the least. Can't you see the loafer is of no value to anyone?

101

Shiri-omo is a word for a loafer. It literally means "heavy ass." On those occasional mornings when I arise before my wife, it is my custom to call to her:

Oi! Shiri-omo-san! Okiro! — Hey, loafer! Get up!

When, however, she is up before I am, she will soothe my sleep-befogged spirits with something like:

*Kono **sodai-gomi** wa mada nete iru ka. Hayaku oki-nasai. Koko wa yōrōin ja arimasen.* — Is this slug-a-bed still asleep? Rise and shine. This is no old folks home. (*Sodai-gomi* means oversized garbage. She's a sweetheart, my wife is. She won my heart the other day when she referred to me in passing as a ***nure-ochiba,*** "a wet leaf," in other words, a listless, lazy one.)

Treachery, Shamelessness, Hypocrisy, Flattery, and Ingratitude

A cornucopia of unsavory traits of character:

on-shirazu — ungrateful wretch
Kono on-shirazu ni muchi no aji wo oshieyō. — I'll give this ungrateful wretch a taste of the whip.
hara-guroi taiko-mochi — scheming toady (lit., a drum-carrier with a black stomach)
Sakki atta otoko wa itsumo chōjō ni peko-peko shite iru. Hara-guroi taiko-mochi da. — The man we met earlier is always dancing attendance on his superiors. He is a scheming toady.

haji-shirazu — shameless
Sono haji-shirazu no on-kise-gamashii taido wa keshikaran.
— The condescending attitude of that shameless fellow
is damnable.

osekkai na gomasuri — meddlesome toadies
*Daitōryō no mawari ni o-sekkai na gomasuri wa ōzei
atsumatte imasu.* — Many meddlesome toadies are
gathered around the president.

uragiri-mono — traitor
gizensha — hypocrite
neko-kaburi — hypocrisy
tsura-yogoshi — disgrace (lit., a face-blackener)
futa-gokoro — treacherous flatterer (lit., two hearts)
chōchin-mochi — a flatterer (lit., a lantern bearer, the
person who went at the head of a group to light the path
for the others)
*Shōtai wo kotowatta yo. Ano yō na futa-gokoro ga aru
chōchin-mochi no apāto ni hairu mon ka.* — I refused
the invitation. Under no circumstances would I enter the
apartment of that treacherous flatterer.

Rascality in General

If you cannot find the zinger you are searching for
among all the preceding, proceed just a little ways further.

seishin no kusatte iru — depraved (lit., spiritually rotten)
*Sono seishin no kusatte iru nariagari-mono wa mainichi
tsura-ate wo iun desu.* — That depraved upstart says
something spiteful every day.
Kono yogore! — You dirty bastard!

darashi no nai — slovenly

Naze sono darashi no nai abazure wo koyō shita ka. — Why did you hire that slovenly wench?

egetsu-nai — vulgar

egetsu-nai gokuaku-nin — vulgar villain of the worst sort

yakubyō-gami — a jinx

Yakubyō-gami da. Issho ni nottara kotchi no kuruma wa kitto jiko wo okosu. — He (she) is a jinx. If he (she) rides in our car, we'll surely have a wreck.

hinekureta seishitsu no hito — someone with a warped mind

kawari-mono — a crank

ijiwaru babā — cantankerous old woman

I hope this book has enabled you to recognize the many forms of direct defamation and has provided you, if attacked, with the weapons to lay about with insulting abuse and hearty curses.